Rumbly tumblies love honey!

Draw a line from each character to his shadow.

Look up, down, across, and diagonally for these words:

POOH	RABBIT
PIGLEt	GOPHER
tIGGER	ROO
EEYORE	KANGA
OWL	BEES

```
S  E  E  B  t  r  R  R  O  O
I  E  O  K  E  F  N  V  W
B  L  E  H  A  t  P  J  W  R
S  M  P  Y  I  N  I  X  O
P  O  W  B  O  C  G  Z  W
G  O  B  N  t  R  L  A  L
Z  A  O  M  C  B  E  H  F
R  Y  U  H  K  L  t  D  t
G  t  I  G  G  E  R  C  P
```

Winnie the Pooh is a happy bear.

Pooh and Piglet are best of friends.

Life is simple in the Hundred-Acre Wood.

Help Pooh and Piglet find their way to Pooh Sticks Bridge.

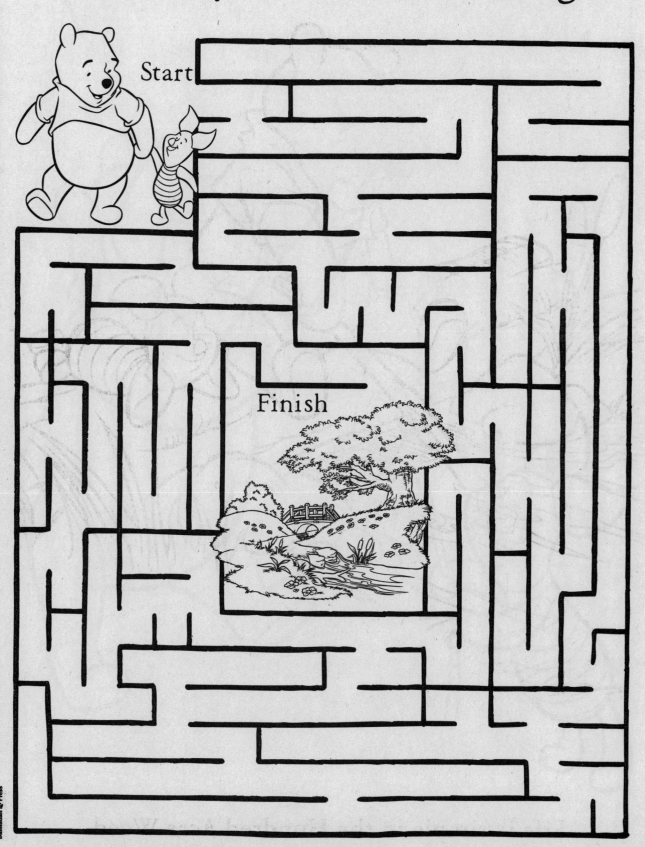

Start

Finish

Make a wish!

Teamwork makes a job more fun.

Tigger is a bouncy pal.

Draw lines from each character to his name.

Pooh   Tigger   Piglet

"Oh, my. There's a rumbly in my tumbly."

Bears love honey!

Honey!

Tiggers like bouncing... not honey!

"Hello, swishy friend!"

"Hello, buddy ol' pal!"

Bears love honey—and so do bees.

Which bee line leads to Pooh's nose?

Your Answer:_____

Rabbit lives in the Hundred-Acre Wood.

How many carrots do you count?

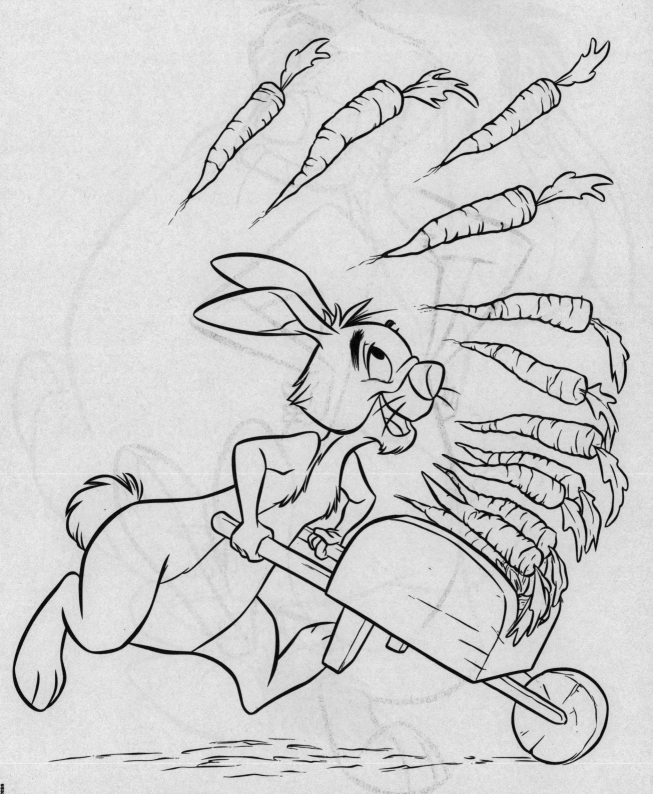

Your Answer: _____

Eeyore can be rather gloomy.

Hidden Pictures

 Circle the hidden bumble bees.

HOW MANY?

Owl lives in a tree house.

Owl likes to give advice.

Kanga is Roo's mother.

How many hops does Roo take to reach Kanga?

Your Answer: _____

Dalmatian Press

A gift from Rabbit.

Which line leads to Tigger?

A   B   C

YOUR ANSWER:

Answer: A

Connect the Dots.

2.

3.

4.

1.

5.

7.

6.

10.

9.

8.

© 2011. Disney

Eeyore brings a box.

Boing-boing-boing!

Small Piglet, big box!

What could Pooh's gift be?

Happy, Happy Day!

Look up, down, across, and diagonally
to find these words.

party   hats
gift   box   yay
present   happy   bows

```
P R E S E N T
P A W I M A F
I O R B O X I
B J S T A H G
H A P P Y A Y
```

Square Off!

Take turns drawing a line between 2 dots (horizontally or vertically).
When a line completes a square, put your initials in it, and take another turn.
When all the dots are connected, the player with the most points wins.
Count 1 point for plain squares, 2 points for squares with Owl,
and 5 points for squares with Pooh.

Player 1 _____   Player 2 _____

Score _____   Score _____

Look, Tigger!

Bear. . . balloon. . .

. . .and bees!

Rabbit is often fretful.

Owl tries to help.

Help Tigger
find his
mirror image
reflection
in the water.

A

B

Your
Answer:

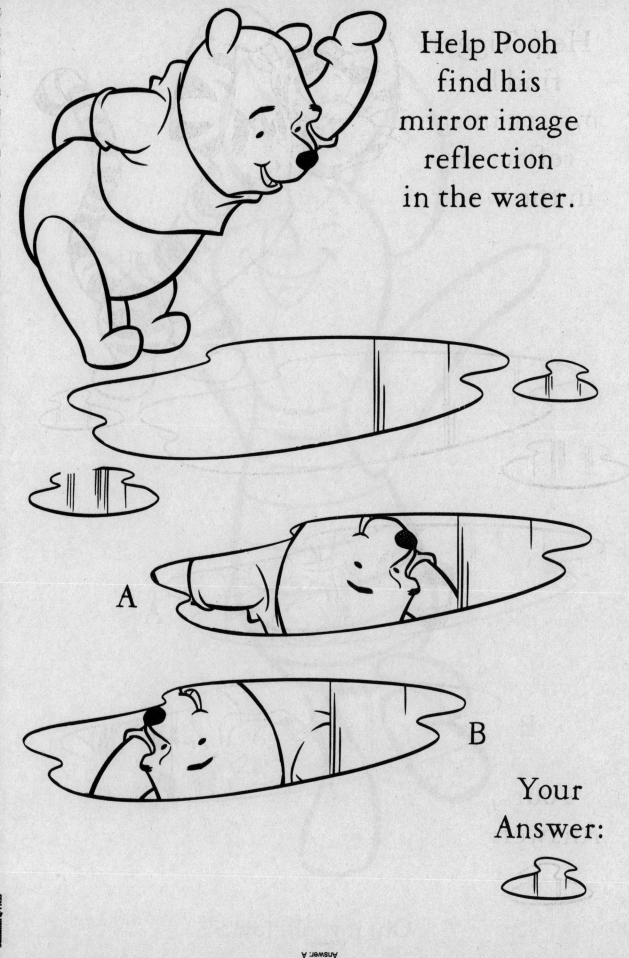

Help Pooh
find his
mirror image
reflection
in the water.

A

B

Your
Answer:

Oh, joy, oh, joy!

Roo wants to play.

"I wonder, I wonder, I wonder..."

"You are wonderfully wonder-filled!"

How many honeypots do you count?

YOUR ANSWER:

Which honeypot is different?

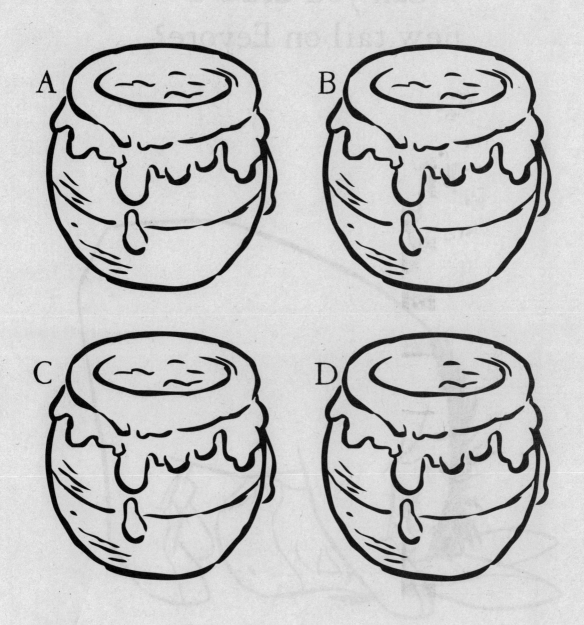

A

B

C

D

YOUR
ANSWER:

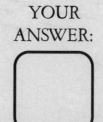

Oh, dear!
Eeyore has lost his tail again!
Can you draw a
new tail on Eeyore?

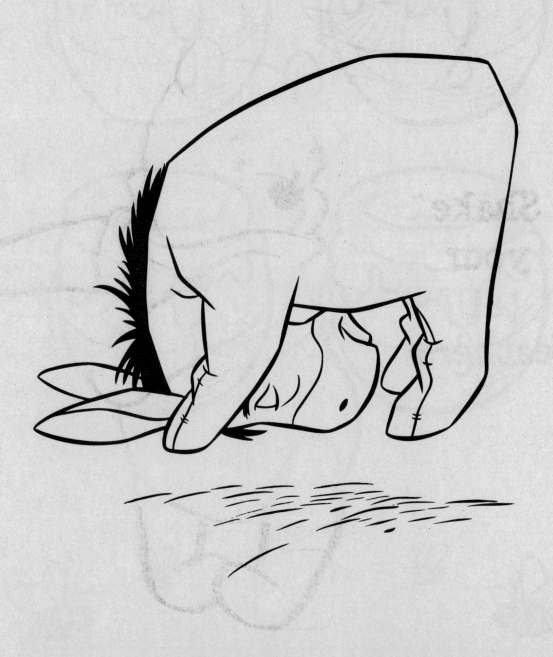

Shake
your
tail
feathers!

Isn't it funny how a bear likes honey?

Piglet is tickled pink.

Pull, Rabbit!

Match each Rabbit to his shadow.

Pooh snoozes.

Which Owl is different?

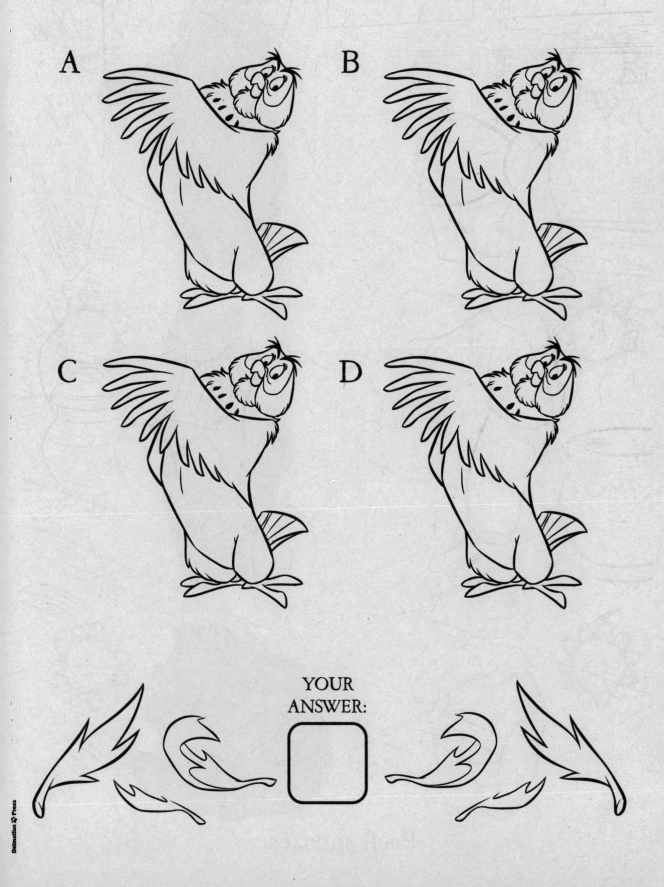

A

B

C

D

YOUR
ANSWER:

Match Pooh to his shadow.

Well, well. . . little acorns!

Lots and lots of acorns!

Color by Number

1 - orange
2 - light pink
3 - dark pink
4 - green
5 - yellow

Find and circle the 5 vegetables that have been added to the picture.

Rabbit gets very cross. . .

...with Tigger!

Pooh has a surprise gift!

Draw a bow on Pooh's gift.

What could owl be saying?

What could Pooh be saying?

What could Pooh be saying?

Good to see you again!

Pooh has a nice, big mirror. Which is Pooh's mirror image?

A

B

C

Your Answer: _____

A little honey would hit the spot.

Where there are bees, there's honey.

Oh, bees! May I have just a bit of honey?

Oh! More than a bit is better!

Pooh has a drifty day.

"Hello, little friend."

Hold on, Piglet!

Wheeeee!

It looks like rain.

Drip-drop!

An umbrella can be a little tent. . .

...or a floaty boat.

Up, up, up!

How many Poohs do you count?

YOUR ANSWER:

Answer: 5

What fun mud can be!

Think, think, think!
Draw what Pooh is thinking about.

In my opinion, a Bear in a chair can float!

Square Off!

Take turns drawing a line between 2 dots (horizontally or vertically).
When a line completes a square, put your initials in it, and take another turn.
When all the dots are connected, the player with the most points wins.
Count 1 point for plain squares, 2 points for squares with Tigger,
and 5 points for squares with Eeyore.

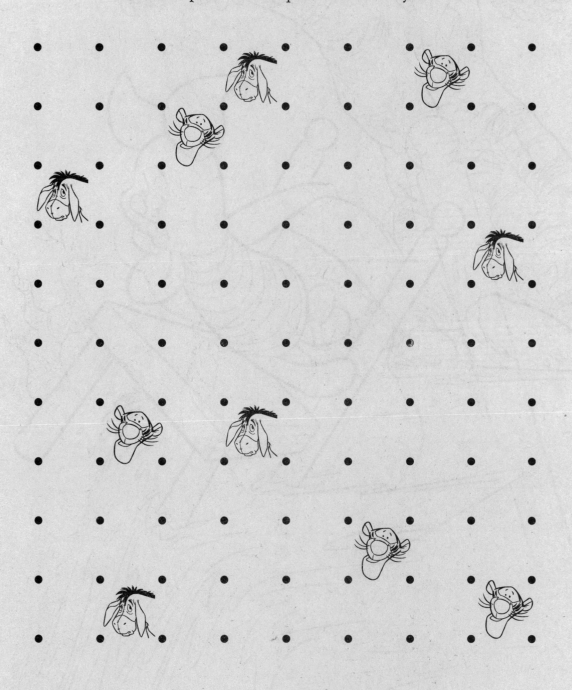

Player 1 _____   Player 2 _____

Score _____   Score _____

Help! Oh, help!

Pooh to the rescue!

Wake up, Pooh!

What a wonderfully blustery day!

Hello, wind!

Piglet is being swept away!

Big wind. Small Piglet!

A boat on the breeze!

Oh dear, oh dearie, dearie, dear!

Draw a kite string from Pooh's hand to the kite.

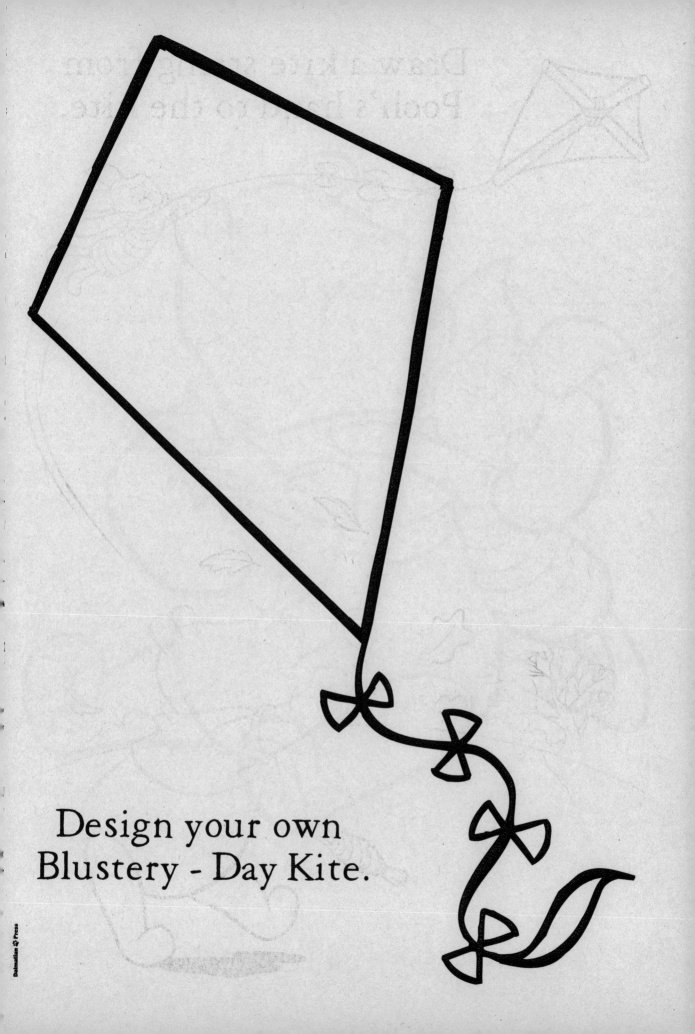

Design your own
Blustery - Day Kite.

A hug is the best gift.

Snuggle up!

What a toasty fire.

Tea with honey is a nice treat.

"Winter is here!"

Here we go

in the snow!

How many snowflakes do you count?

Your Answer:_____

A fine day for skating!

Follow the tracks...

...where do they go?

Slippity-slide...

...Slippity day!

Rain, rain, come and play!

Draw

Tigger in the frame below.

Which Piglet is different?

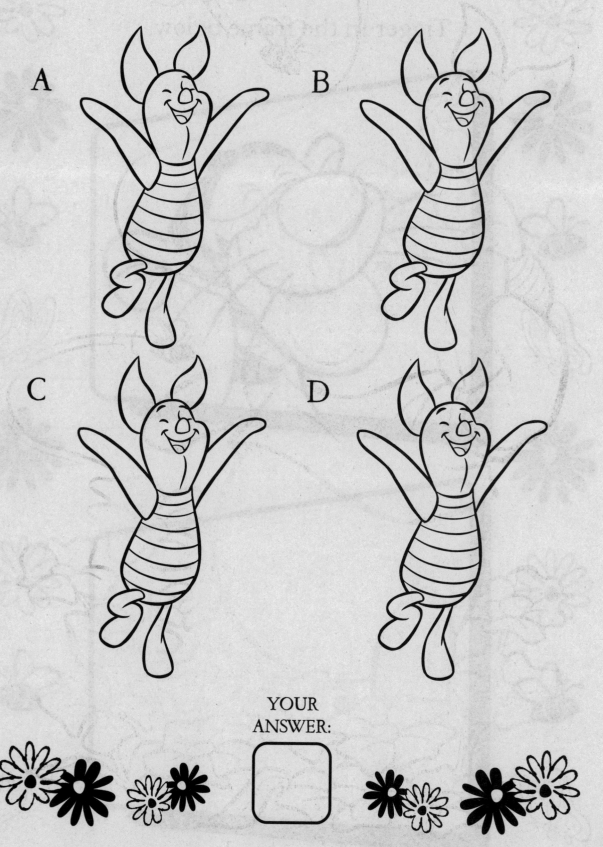

A

B

C

D

YOUR
ANSWER:

Answer: A

It's spring!

"Hello, flutter-friend!"

Which two pictures are the same?

A

B

C

D

YOUR ANSWERS:

☐ & ☐

Answer: B & C

Which carrot is different?

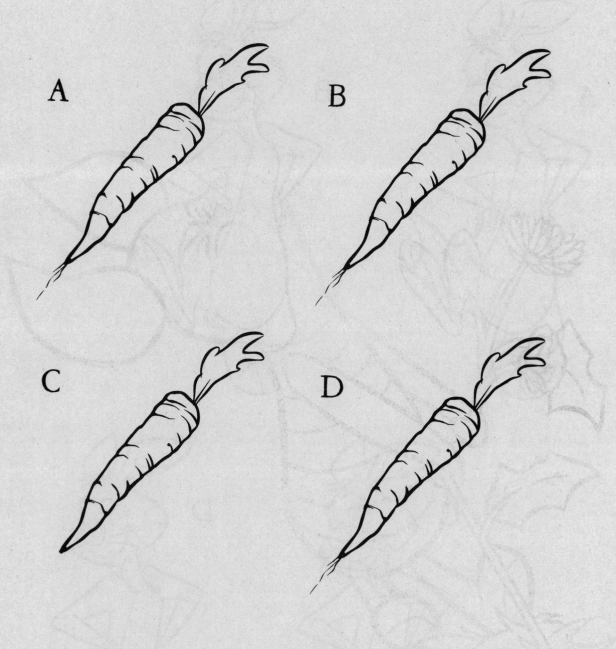

A

B

C

D

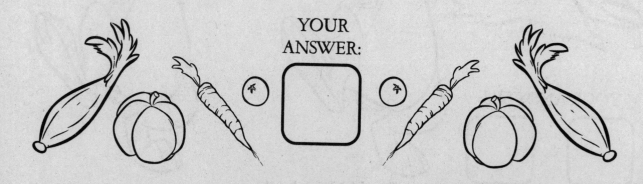

YOUR
ANSWER:

Pull, Piglet!

Which Pooh picture is different?

A

B

C

D

YOUR
ANSWER:

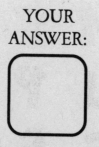

Look up, down, across, and diagonally for these words:

FOREST   LEAF

TREE   FLOWER

BIRD   RABBIT

WOOD   BEAR

t t B I P E S O O O

B R O I E K F t B

N A E I R t L L E

S B G E Z D O X A

D B W B O C W Z R

O I L E A F E N L

O t Z M C B R H R

W M B U P L t S E

F O R E S t R C B

Find your way through the
Hundred-Acre Wood
to Eeyore.

Start

Finish

A pinwheel for Piglet.

Color by Number

1: blue   3: green   5: purple
2: yellow   4: red   6: orange

Think, think, think!
Draw what Pooh is looking at.

Connect the Dots.

How many words can you make from the letters in:

A bother free day

_____

_____

_____

_____

Look up, down, across, and diagonally for these words:

FISH   WORM
POND   TURTLE
NET   LILYPAD
WATER   FUN

t	t	B	I	P	E	T	O	P
U	R	O	I	E	K	E	t	O
R	A	F	I	R	t	N	L	N
t	L	I	L	Y	P	A	D	D
L	B	S	B	O	C	W	Z	R
E	I	H	W	A	T	E	R	M
F	t	Z	O	C	B	R	H	R
W	U	B	N	P	L	t	S	O
W	F	O	N	D	S	t	R	C	W

Use the grid to draw Eeyore.

Color the seasons!

Fall

Winter

Spring

Summer

Look at the picture and these 5 pieces.
Which 3 pieces complete the picture?

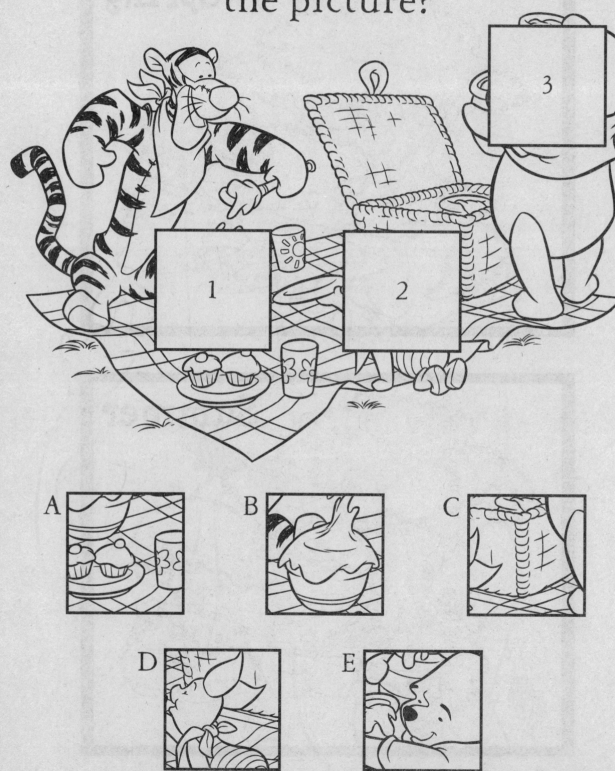

Answer: 1-B, 2-D, 3-E

Connect the Dots.

Owl suggests an adventure.

Hooray, hooray! On our way!

Piglet finds a fluttery bush.

Oh, me, oh, my!

"Not that way, Tigger!"

This way!

What's ahead?

Rabbit is befuddled.

Pooh is puzzled.

Look Out!
Study these two pages.

Circle 5 things that are different in this picture.

Answers: Pooh is facing the other way, Piglet's left arm, Rabbit's tail, Tigger and Eeyore have switched places, Eeyore's missing his tail

Whoa!

Oh, my, oh, my!

Hang on!

How many bees
are after Pooh's honey?

YOUR ANSWER:

Oof!

Whee!

Which line leads to Eeyore?

YOUR ANSWER:

Tic-Tac-Toe

"If there's a cloud, it finds me."

What a friendly little shower!

Match each owl to his shadow.

This is Rabbit's rabbit hole.

Hello, Rabbit!

Pooh likes to eat lots of honey.

Too much honey makes for a pudgy Pooh!

Tic-Tac-Toe

Push! Push!

Rabbit is creative!

Which piece completes the picture?

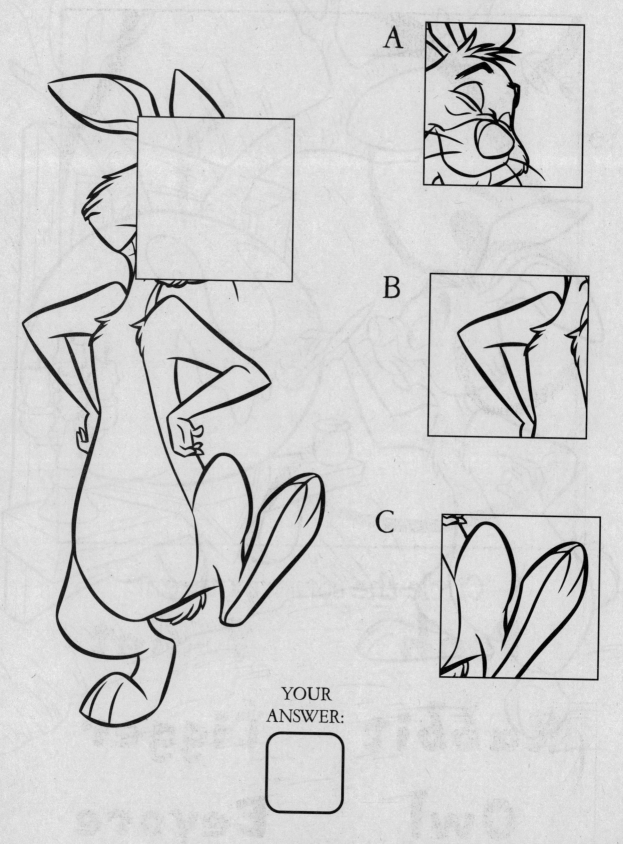

A

B

C

YOUR
ANSWER:

Answer: A

WHO AM I?

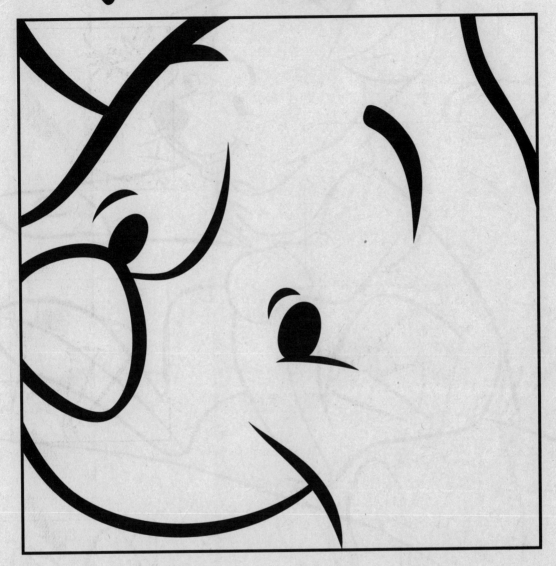

Circle the correct answer.

Pooh   Piglet

Rabbit   tigger

Owl   Eeyore

Roo is up in a tree.

Color by Number

1: yellow
2: red
3: blue

Oh dear, oh dearie, dearie dear!"

Tiggers are very down-to-earth.

Eeyore fixes his house. . . again.

Even Eeyore can be silly.

Oopsy-daisy!
Study these two pages.

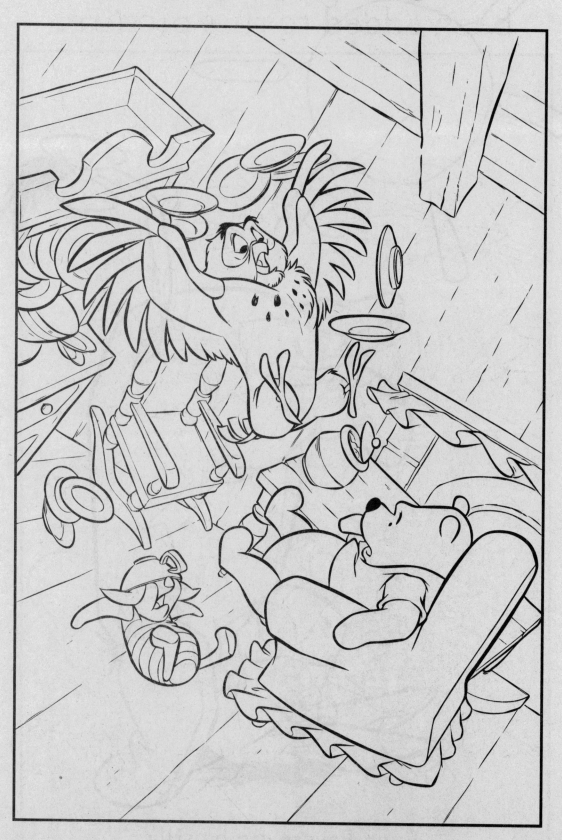

Topsy-turvy!
Circle 5 things that have
been added to this picture.

A snooze for two.

Piglet is giggly over missing his middle.
Connect the dots to finish Piglet.

Look Out!
Study these two pages.

Circle 5 things that are different in this picture.

Answers: Tigger is different; Piglet is moved; Leaves missing from branch at bottom; Plant missing from water; Lines missing from tree

Tigger bounces through the Hundred-Acre Wood.

"Who wants to play Hide-and-Seek?"

Hoo-hoo! Where are you?

Where should we hide from Tigger now?

Maybe this lookity-out tree is too high.

Hoo-hoo! I found you!

Draw a line from each character to his shadow.

Boing! Boing! March!

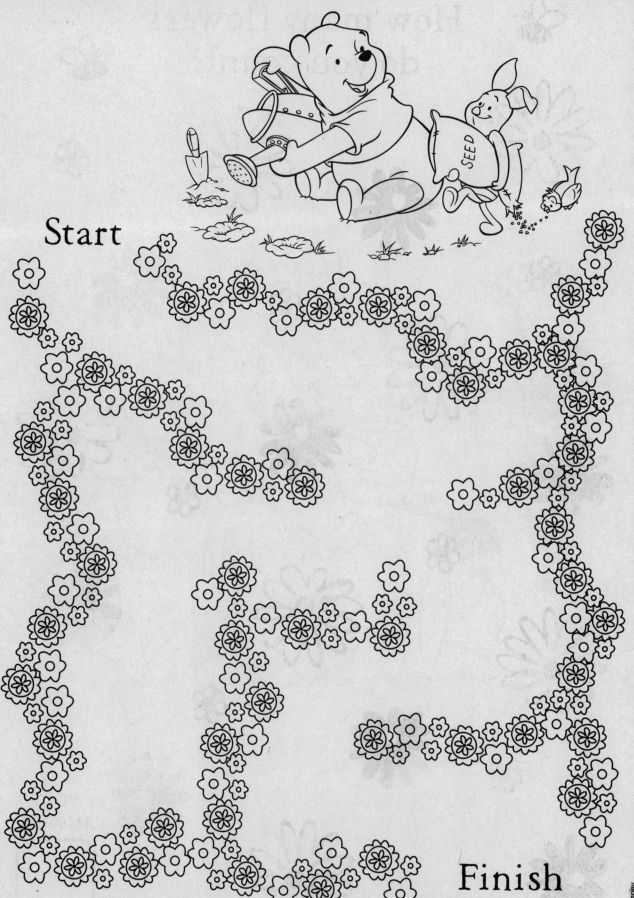

Start

Finish

How many flowers
do you count?

YOUR
ANSWER:

What a honey good time!